Incredible
Gluten-Free
recipes

Publications International, Ltd.

# HOW TO EAT GLUTEN-FREE AND LOVE IT

### What Is Gluten Anyway?

Gluten is a protein that is found in wheat, rye and barley. There are many reasons people avoid gluten. Celiac disease is the most serious. There are others who have a sensitivity to gluten and just feel better when they avoid it. Some people are allergic to wheat itself. You know which category you belong in if you're reading this book!

### No More Bread? No Pasta?

At first, going gluten-free may sound awfully limiting. Fortunately, there are many more delicious foods on the gluten-free list than the forbidden list. There are also more and more products, from cereals to baking mixes to pastas, which are now being formulated in gluten-free versions. These days you'll find them not just in health food stores and online, but also on the shelves of most major supermarkets.

### Some Good News

Spotting hidden gluten in processed foods is a lot easier now thanks to the FDA's Food Allergy Labeling Law that went into effect in 2004. Since wheat is a common allergen, any product that contains wheat or is derived from it must say so on the label. That means formerly questionable ingredients, such as modified food starch or maltodextrin, must now show wheat as part of their name if they were made from it (for example, "wheat maltodextrin"). Be aware that this ONLY applies to foods produced in the US and Canada. Imports are a different matter.

### More Good News

Look at your dietary restrictions as an opportunity to try new foods. Add quinoa and chickpea flour to your cupboard. Use corn tortillas to make sandwiches or lasagna. You'll find easy recipes in this book that are so delicious you'll forget that they're gluten-free. Healthy eating may actually be easier without gluten, too. Adding more fresh produce to your meals, eating less processed food and avoiding refined flour are all steps to a better diet for anyone.

## The Short List

Sensitivities differ from person to person and ingredients differ from brand to brand. Always check the label's fine print. This is an abbreviated list of some of the most commonly used items.

| •Red Lights• (contain gluten) | •Yellow Lights• (check ingredients) | •Green Lights• (no gluten) |
|---|---|---|
| barley | flavorings and fillers | beans |
| beer | frozen vegetables with sauces/seasonings | buckwheat |
| blue cheese | | cellophane noodles* |
| bulgur | marinades | chickpea flour** |
| cereal | mustard | corn |
| commercial baked goods | salad dressings | dairy |
| | soups | eggs |
| couscous | soy sauce* | fresh fruits |
| durum | *most are made with wheat | fresh vegetables |
| graham | | lentils |
| gravies and sauces | | meat & poultry |
| imitation seafood | | millet |
| malt, malt flavoring and malt vinegar | | nuts |
| | | potatoes |
| oats* | | quinoa |
| pizza | | rice |
| pretzels | | rice noodles |
| rye | | seafood |
| seitan | | soy |
| semolina | | tapioca |
| spelt | | tofu |
| wheat | | |

*because they are processed in facilities with wheat

*also called bean thread noodles

**garbanzo flour

# Smart Starts

## Ham & Potato Pancakes

¾ **pound Yukon gold potatoes, peeled, grated and squeezed dry (about 2 cups)**
¼ **cup finely chopped green onions**
2 **eggs, beaten**
1 **cup (4 to 5 ounces) finely chopped cooked ham**
¼ **cup rice flour**
¼ **teaspoon salt**
¼ **teaspoon black pepper**
2 **to 3 tablespoons vegetable oil**
   **Chili sauce or mild fruit chutney (optional)**

1. Combine potatoes, green onions and eggs in large bowl; mix well. Add ham, rice flour, salt and pepper; mix well.

2. Heat 2 tablespoons oil in large heavy skillet over medium-high heat. Drop batter by heaping tablespoonfuls and press with back of spoon to flatten. Cook 2 to 3 minutes per side. Remove to paper towels to drain. Add remaining 1 tablespoon oil, if necessary, to cook remaining batter. Serve pancakes with chili sauce.

*Makes 4 servings (4 pancakes each)*

### *Tip

Rice flour can often be substituted for regular all-purpose flour in recipes like this one. If a small amount of flour is called for to bind ingredients together, rice flour works just as well as regular flour. Use either brown or white rice flour. Brown rice flour, like the brown rice it is made from, has a slightly better nutritional profile.

# Apple-Cinnamon Breakfast Risotto

¼ cup (½ stick) butter
4 medium Granny Smith apples, diced (about 1½ pounds)
1½ teaspoons ground cinnamon
¼ teaspoon ground allspice
¼ teaspoon salt
1½ cups arborio rice
½ cup packed dark brown sugar
4 cups unfiltered apple juice,* at room temperature
1 teaspoon vanilla
Sliced almonds and dried cherries (optional)
Milk (optional)

*If unfiltered apple juice is unavailable, use any apple juice.*

**Slow Cooker Directions**

1. Coat slow cooker with nonstick cooking spray. Melt butter in large skillet over medium-high heat. Add apples, cinnamon, allspice and salt. Cook and stir 3 to 5 minutes or until apples begin to release juices. Transfer to slow cooker.

2. Add rice and stir to coat. Sprinkle with brown sugar; add apple juice and vanilla. Cover; cook on HIGH 1½ to 2 hours or until all liquid is absorbed. Ladle risotto into bowls and serve hot. Top with almonds and cherries and drizzle with milk, if desired.

*Makes 6 servings*

# Smoked Salmon Hash Browns

**3 cups frozen hash brown potatoes, thawed**
**2 pouches (3 ounces each) smoked salmon\***
**½ cup chopped onion**
**½ cup chopped green bell pepper**
**¼ teaspoon black pepper**
**2 tablespoons vegetable oil**

*\*Smoked salmon in foil pouches can be found in the canned fish section of the supermarket. Do not substitute lox or other fresh smoked salmon.*

1. Combine potatoes, salmon, onion, bell pepper and black pepper in large bowl; mix well.

2. Heat oil in large skillet over medium-high heat. Add potato mixture; pat down evenly in skillet.

3. Cook 5 minutes or until bottom is crisp. Turn over in large pieces. Cook 2 to 3 minutes or until both sides are browned.

*Makes 4 servings*

# Cornmeal Pancakes

**2 cups buttermilk**
**2 eggs, lightly beaten**
**¼ cup sugar**
**2 tablespoons butter, melted**
**1 cup yellow cornmeal**
**¼ cup gluten-free all-purpose flour blend**
**1 teaspoon salt**
**1 teaspoon baking powder**
**½ teaspoon baking soda**
**Blueberries (optional)**

1. Combine buttermilk, eggs, sugar and butter in large bowl; beat until well blended. Combine cornmeal, gluten-free flour, salt, baking powder and baking soda in medium bowl; stir into buttermilk mixture. Let stand 5 minutes.

2. Lightly grease griddle or large skillet; place over medium heat. Drop about 2 tablespoons batter onto hot griddle for each pancake. Cook about 3 minutes or until tops of pancakes are bubbly and appear dry; turn and cook about 2 minutes or until bottoms are golden. Serve with blueberries, if desired.  *Makes 4 servings*

*Tip

Most gluten-free flours and flour mixes should be stored in the freezer if you won't be using them up quickly. Store them in resealable freezer bags and allow the contents to come to room temperature before measuring and using them.

# Wild Rice & Pepper Frittata

**1 tablespoon olive oil**
**1 large shallot, minced**
**1 clove garlic, minced**
**1 cup chopped shiitake mushrooms***
**1 large roasted red bell pepper, chopped**
**1 cup cooked wild rice**
**½ teaspoon salt, divided**
**¼ teaspoon black pepper, divided**
**⅛ teaspoon ground paprika**
**6 eggs**
**¼ cup shredded Asiago cheese**

*If shiitake mushrooms are not available, use any mushroom variety.*

1. Preheat broiler. Heat oil in large nonstick ovenproof skillet. Add shallot and garlic. Cook and stir over medium heat 1 minute. Add mushrooms; cook and stir 5 minutes or until tender. Stir in red pepper, wild rice, ¼ teaspoon salt, ⅛ teaspoon black pepper and paprika. Cook and stir over high heat 1 minute or until any liquid evaporates. Remove from heat.

2. Beat eggs in large bowl with remaining ¼ teaspoon salt and ⅛ teaspoon black pepper. Pour eggs into skillet; tilt to spread over rice. Cook over medium heat until eggs are set but still glossy. Sprinkle with cheese.

3. Broil 3 to 4 minutes or until cheese melts and frittata edges are browned. Let rest 2 to 3 minutes to firm up.     *Makes 6 servings*

**\*Tip**

To roast a fresh red bell pepper, place it on a stovetop over an open flame or 4 inches from heat in a broiler. Turn frequently to blacken all sides, using long-handled tongs. Place the blackened pepper in a paper or plastic bag, shut the bag and set it aside for 30 minutes to 1 hour to loosen the pepper's skin. Scrape off the blackened skin with a paring knife.

# Cheese Grits with Chiles & Bacon

**6 strips bacon**
**1 serrano or jalapeño pepper,\* minced**
**1 large shallot or small onion, finely chopped**
**4 cups chicken broth**
**1 cup uncooked grits\*\***
**¼ teaspoon black pepper**
   **Salt**
**1 cup (4 ounces) shredded Cheddar cheese**
**½ cup half-and-half**
**2 tablespoons finely chopped green onion**

*\*Hot peppers can sting and irritate the skin, so wear rubber gloves when handling peppers and do not touch your eyes.*

*\*\*You may use coarse, instant, yellow or stone-ground grits.*

## Slow Cooker Directions

1. Cook bacon in medium skillet until crisp. Remove bacon and drain on paper towels. Crumble 2 strips and place in slow cooker. Refrigerate and reserve remaining bacon.

2. Drain all but 1 tablespoon bacon drippings from skillet. Add serrano pepper and shallot. Cook and stir over medium-high heat 1 minute or until shallot is transparent and lightly browned. Transfer to slow cooker. Stir in broth, grits, pepper and salt. Cover; cook on LOW 4 hours.

3. Stir in cheese and half-and-half. Sprinkle with green onion. Crumble reserved bacon over grits.                    *Makes 4 servings*

# Goat Cheese & Tomato Omelet

**3 egg whites**
**2 eggs**
**1 tablespoon water**
**⅛ teaspoon salt**
**⅛ teaspoon black pepper**
   **Nonstick cooking spray**
**⅓ cup crumbled goat cheese**
**1 medium plum tomato, diced (⅓ cup)**
**2 tablespoons chopped fresh basil or parsley**

1. Whisk together egg whites, eggs, water, salt and pepper in medium bowl.

2. Spray medium nonstick skillet with cooking spray; place over medium heat. Add egg mixture; cook 2 minutes or until eggs begin to set on bottom. Gently lift edges of omelet to allow uncooked portion to flow underneath. Cook 3 minutes or until center is almost set.

3. Sprinkle cheese, tomato and basil over half of omelet. Fold omelet over filling. Continue cooking 1 to 2 minutes or until cheese begins to melt and center is set.                *Makes 2 servings*

**\*Tip**

Omelets cook very quickly so make sure you have the filling ingredients ready to go before you start cooking the eggs. Don't think of omelets only as a breakfast items. They make nutritious, quick and easy lunches or dinners and are a great way to use up small amounts of leftover cooked vegetables or meats.

# Small Plates

## Socca (Niçoise Chickpea Pancake)

**1 cup chickpea flour***
**¾ teaspoon salt**
**½ teaspoon ground pepper**
**1 cup water**
**5 tablespoons olive oil, divided**
**1½ teaspoons minced fresh basil *or* ½ teaspoon dried basil**
**1 teaspoon minced fresh rosemary *or* ¼ teaspoon dried rosemary**
**¼ teaspoon dried thyme**

*\*Chickpea flour is also called garbanzo flour. It is found in the specialty food section of most supermarkets.*

1. Sift chickpea flour into medium bowl. Stir in salt and pepper. Gradually whisk in water to create a smooth batter. Stir in 2 tablespoons olive oil. Allow batter to rest at least 30 minutes.

2. Preheat oven to 450°F about 10 minutes before ready to bake socca. Place 9- or 10-inch cast iron skillet in oven to heat.

3. Add basil, rosemary and thyme to batter; whisk until smooth. Carefully remove skillet from oven using oven mitts. Add 2 tablespoons olive oil to skillet; swirl to coat evenly. Immediately pour in batter.

4. Bake socca 12 to 15 minutes or until edge begins to pull away and center is firm. Remove skillet; turn oven to broil.

5. Brush socca with remaining 1 tablespoon oil and broil 2 to 4 minutes until dark brown in spots. Cut into wedges and serve warm. *Makes 6 servings*

# Mini Carnitas Tacos

1½ pounds boneless pork loin, cut into 1-inch cubes
1 onion, finely chopped
½ cup reduced-sodium chicken broth
1 tablespoon chili powder
2 teaspoons ground cumin
1 teaspoon dried oregano
½ teaspoon minced chipotle chile in adobo sauce (optional)
½ cup pico de gallo or salsa
2 tablespoons chopped fresh cilantro
½ teaspoon salt
12 (6-inch) corn tortillas
¾ cup (3 ounces) shredded sharp Cheddar cheese
3 tablespoons sour cream

## Slow Cooker Directions

1. Combine pork, onion, broth, chili powder, cumin, oregano and chipotle chile, if desired, in slow cooker. Cover; cook on LOW 6 hours or on HIGH 3 hours or until pork is very tender. Pour off excess cooking liquid.

2. Shred pork with 2 forks; stir in pico de gallo, cilantro and salt. Cover and keep warm.

3. Cut 3 circles from each tortilla with 2-inch biscuit cutter. Top with pork, cheese and sour cream. Serve warm.

*Makes 12 servings (36 mini tacos)*

### *Tip

Carnitas means "little meats" in Spanish. The dish is usually made with an inexpensive cut of pork that is simmered for a long time until it is so tender it falls into pieces. Then the meat is browned in pork fat. The slow cooker makes the long, slow cooking process easy to manage and skipping the final browning lowers the fat content.

# Zucchini with
## Toasted Chickpea Flour

**½ cup sifted chickpea flour**
**1½ pounds zucchini or summer squash (3 or 4 squash)**
**2 tablespoons olive oil**
**1 tablespoon butter**
**3 teaspoons minced garlic**
**1 teaspoon salt**
**½ teaspoon pepper**
**½ cup water**

1. Heat small skillet over medium-high heat; add chickpea flour. Cook and stir 3 to 4 minutes until fragrant and slightly darker in color. Remove from skillet; set aside.

2. Cut zucchini into ½-inch-thick circles or half moons. Heat oil and butter in large skillet. Cook and stir garlic 1 minute or until fragrant. Add zucchini, salt and pepper; cook and stir 5 minutes or until beginning to soften.

3. Stir chickpea flour into skillet to coat zucchini. Pour in water; cook and stir 2 to 3 minutes or until moist crumbs form, scraping bottom of skillet frequently to prevent sticking and scrape up brown bits. *Makes 4 servings*

### *Tip

Using chickpea flour to add substance and nutrition to vegetable dishes is a method adapted from Indian cuisine. The flour forms delicious, nutty crumbs that become part of the dish. The same method can be used with other vegetables as well.

# Quinoa & Mango Salad

**1 cup uncooked quinoa***
**2 cups water**
**2 cups cubed peeled mango (about 2 large mangoes)**
**½ cup sliced green onions**
**½ cup dried cranberries**
**2 tablespoons chopped fresh parsley**
**¼ cup olive oil**
**1 tablespoon plus 1½ teaspoons white wine vinegar**
**1 teaspoon Dijon mustard**
**½ teaspoon salt**
**⅛ teaspoon black pepper**

*Pronounced keen-wah. This grain is available in health food stores or in the health food aisle of large supermarkets.*

1. Place quinoa in fine-mesh strainer; rinse well. Transfer to medium saucepan and add water. Bring to a boil. Reduce heat; simmer, covered, 10 to 12 minutes until all water is absorbed. Stir; let stand, covered, 15 minutes. Transfer to large bowl; cover and refrigerate at least 1 hour.

2. Add mango, green onions, cranberries and parsley to quinoa; mix well.

3. Combine oil, vinegar, mustard, salt and pepper in small bowl; whisk until blended. Pour over quinoa mixture; mix until well blended.                    *Makes 8 (⅔-cup) servings*

### *Tip

While quinoa is an ancient grain that was grown by Incas, it is new to most Americans. This tiny round whole grain is higher in protein than other grains including wheat. It contains all eight essential amino acids; therefore, it is considered a complete protein.

# Thai Salad Rolls with Spicy Sweet & Sour Sauce

**Spicy Sweet & Sour Sauce (recipe follows)**
**3 ounces thin rice noodles (rice vermicelli)**
**4 ounces large raw shrimp, peeled and deveined**
**1 medium cucumber, seeded and cut into matchstick pieces**
**½ cup fresh cilantro leaves**
**½ cup fresh mint leaves**
**1 large bunch green leaf lettuce**

1. Prepare Spicy Sweet & Sour Sauce; set aside. Soak noodles in hot water 10 minutes to soften. Rinse under cold running water; drain.

2. Bring water to a boil in medium saucepan. Add shrimp; return to a boil. Cook 3 to 5 minutes or until shrimp turn pink and opaque; drain. When cool, cut each shrimp lengthwise in half.

3. Arrange shrimp, noodles, cucumber, cilantro and mint in center of lettuce leaves and roll up. Serve with Spicy Sweet & Sour Sauce.

*Makes 6 servings*

## Spicy Sweet & Sour Sauce

**2 tablespoons rice vinegar**
**1 tablespoon cornstarch**
**¾ cup water**
**¼ cup packed brown sugar**
**½ teaspoon red pepper flakes**
**1 green onion, minced**

Combine vinegar and cornstarch in small bowl; mix well. Combine water, brown sugar, pepper flakes and green onion in small saucepan; bring to a boil. Stir in cornstarch mixture. Return to a boil; cook 1 minute or until sauce is clear and thickened. Cool.

# Curried Noodles

**7 ounces thin rice noodles (rice vermicelli)**
**1 tablespoon peanut or vegetable oil**
**1 large red bell pepper, cut into short, thin strips**
**2 green onions, cut into ½-inch pieces**
**1 clove garlic, minced**
**1 teaspoon minced fresh ginger**
**2 teaspoons curry powder**
**⅛ to ¼ teaspoon red pepper flakes**
**½ cup vegetable broth**
**2 tablespoons gluten-free soy sauce**

1. Place noodles in bowl; cover with boiling water. Soak 15 minutes to soften. Drain; cut into 3-inch pieces.

2. Heat oil in wok or large skillet over medium-high heat. Add bell pepper strips; stir-fry 3 minutes.

3. Add onions, garlic and ginger; stir-fry 1 minute. Add curry powder and red pepper flakes; stir-fry 1 minute.

4. Add broth and soy sauce; cook and stir 2 minutes. Add noodles; cook and stir 3 minutes or until heated through.

*Makes 6 servings*

**\*Tip**

Asian rice noodles are a great go-to for gluten-free diets. Most are made of rice flour and water. Rice noodles come in various widths and are sometimes labeled rice sticks or rice vermicelli. Do check labels carefully, though, since some rice noodles can have wheat flour as an ingredient as well.

# Quinoa-Stuffed Tomatoes

½ **cup uncooked quinoa**
1 **cup water**
½ **teaspoon salt, divided**
1 **tablespoon olive oil**
1 **red bell pepper, chopped**
⅓ **cup chopped green onion**
⅛ **teaspoon black pepper**
⅛ **teaspoon dried thyme**
1 **tablespoon butter**
8 **plum tomatoes,\* halved lengthwise, seeded, hollowed out**

*\*Or substitute 4 medium tomatoes.*

1. Preheat oven to 325°F. Place quinoa in fine-mesh strainer; rinse well. Bring water and ¼ teaspoon salt to a boil in small saucepan. Stir in quinoa. Cover; reduce heat to low. Simmer 12 to 14 minutes or until quinoa is tender and water is absorbed.

2. Heat oil in large skillet over medium-high heat. Add bell pepper; cook and stir 7 to 10 minutes or until tender. Stir in quinoa, green onion, remaining ¼ teaspoon salt, black pepper and thyme. Add butter; stir until melted.

3. Arrange tomato halves in baking dish. Fill with quinoa mixture. Bake 15 to 20 minutes or until tomatoes are tender.

*Makes 8 servings*

# Asparagus-Parmesan Risotto

**5½ cups vegetable broth**
**4 tablespoons unsalted butter, divided**
**⅓ cup finely chopped onion**
**2 cups uncooked arborio rice**
**⅔ cup dry white wine**
**2½ cups fresh asparagus pieces (about 1 inch long)**
**⅔ cup peas**
**Salt and black pepper**
**1 cup grated Parmesan cheese**

1. Bring broth to a boil in medium saucepan over medium-high heat; reduce heat to low and simmer.

2. Meanwhile, melt 3 tablespoons butter in large saucepan over medium heat. Add onion; cook and stir 2 to 3 minutes or until tender. Add rice; cook and stir 2 minutes. Add wine; cook, stirring occasionally, until most of wine is absorbed.

3. Add 1½ cups broth; cook and stir 6 to 7 minutes or until most of liquid is absorbed. (Mixture should simmer, but not boil.) Add 2 cups broth and asparagus; cook and stir 6 to 7 minutes or until most of liquid is absorbed. Add remaining 2 cups broth and peas; cook and stir 5 to 6 minutes or until most of liquid is absorbed and rice mixture is creamy. Season with salt and black pepper.

4. Remove from heat; stir in remaining 1 tablespoon butter and Parmesan cheese until melted.                    *Makes 4 to 5 servings*

**Asparagus-Spinach Risotto:** Substitute 1 cup baby spinach leaves or chopped large spinach leaves for peas. Add spinach at the end of step 3; cover and let stand 1 minute or until spinach is wilted.

**Asparagus-Chicken Risotto:** Add 2 cups chopped or shredded cooked chicken to risotto with peas in step 3. Proceed as directed.

## Gluten-Free Pizza

1¾ cups gluten-free all-purpose flour blend
1½ cups white rice flour
2 teaspoons sugar
1 envelope (¼ ounce) rapid-rise yeast
1½ teaspoons salt
1½ teaspoons Italian seasoning
1 teaspoon baking powder
½ teaspoon xanthan gum*
1¼ cups hot water (120°F)
2 tablespoons olive oil
Toppings: pizza sauce, fresh mozzarella, sliced
tomatoes, fresh basil, grated Parmesan cheese

*Available in health food stores and near other gluten-free items in most supermarkets.*

1. Combine all dry ingredients in bowl of stand mixer. With mixer running on low speed, add water in steady stream until soft dough ball forms. Add olive oil and beat 2 minutes. Transfer to rice-floured surface and knead 2 minutes or until dough holds together in a smooth ball.

2. Place dough in oiled bowl; turn to coat. Cover; let rise 30 minutes in warm place. (Dough will increase in size but not double.)

3. Preheat oven to 400°F. Line pizza pan or baking sheet with foil. Punch down dough and transfer to center of prepared pan. Spread dough as thin as possible (about ⅛ inch thick) using dampened hands. Bake 5 to 7 minutes or until crust begins to color. (Crust may crack in spots.)

4. Top pizza with favorite toppings. Bake 10 to 15 minutes or until cheese is melted and pizza is cooked through.

*Makes 4 to 6 servings*

# Fiesta Beef Enchiladas

**2 sheets (20×12 inches) heavy-duty foil, generously sprayed with nonstick cooking spray**
**6 ounces ground beef**
**¼ cup sliced green onions**
**1 teaspoon minced garlic**
**1 cup (4 ounces) shredded Mexican cheese blend or Cheddar cheese, divided**
**¾ cup chopped tomato, divided**
**½ cup corn**
**½ cup black beans**
**⅓ cup cooked white or brown rice**
**¼ cup salsa or picante sauce**
**6 (6-inch) corn tortillas**
**½ cup gluten-free red or green enchilada sauce**
**½ cup sliced romaine lettuce**

1. Preheat oven to 375°F. Brown ground beef in large nonstick skillet over medium-high heat, stirring to separate meat. Drain fat. Add green onions and garlic; cook and stir 2 minutes.

2. Combine meat mixture, ¾ cup cheese, ½ cup tomato, corn, beans, rice and salsa; mix well. Spoon mixture down center of tortillas. Roll up; place 3 enchiladas, seam side down, on each foil sheet. Spoon enchilada sauce evenly over enchiladas.

3. Double fold sides and ends of foil to seal packets, leaving head space for heat circulation. Place packets on baking sheet.

4. Bake 15 minutes. Remove from oven; open packets. Sprinkle with remaining ¼ cup cheese; reseal packets. Bake 10 minutes more. Transfer enchiladas to serving plates; serve with lettuce and remaining ¼ cup tomato. *Makes 2 servings*

# Pad Thai

8 ounces uncooked rice noodles (rice vermicelli)
2 tablespoons unseasoned rice wine vinegar
1½ tablespoons fish sauce*
1 to 2 tablespoons fresh lemon juice
1 tablespoon ketchup
2 teaspoons sugar
¼ teaspoon red pepper flakes
1 tablespoon vegetable oil
1 boneless skinless chicken breast (about 4 ounces),
   finely chopped
2 green onions, thinly sliced
2 cloves garlic, minced
3 ounces small raw shrimp, peeled
2 cups fresh bean sprouts
¾ cup shredded red cabbage
1 medium carrot, shredded
3 tablespoons minced fresh cilantro
2 tablespoons chopped unsalted dry-roasted peanuts
   Lime wedges

*Fish sauce is available at most large supermarkets and Asian markets.*

1. Place noodles in medium bowl. Cover with boiling water; let soak 30 minutes or until soft. Drain and set aside. Combine vinegar, fish sauce, lemon juice, ketchup, sugar and red pepper flakes in small bowl.

2. Heat oil in wok or large nonstick skillet over medium-high heat. Add chicken, green onions and garlic. Cook and stir until chicken is no longer pink. Stir in noodles; cook 1 minute. Add shrimp; cook about 3 minutes, just until shrimp turn pink and opaque. Stir in fish sauce mixture; toss to coat evenly. Add bean sprouts and cook until heated through, about 2 minutes.

3. Serve with shredded cabbage, carrot, cilantro, peanuts and lime wedges.                                    *Makes 5 servings*

# Roast Turkey Breast with Sausage & Apple Stuffing

**8 ounces bulk pork sausage**
**1 medium apple, peeled and finely chopped**
**1 shallot or small onion, finely chopped**
**1 stalk celery, finely chopped**
**¼ cup chopped hazelnuts**
**½ teaspoon rubbed sage, divided**
**½ teaspoon salt, divided**
**½ teaspoon black pepper, divided**
**1 tablespoon butter, softened**
**1 whole boneless turkey breast (4½ to 5 pounds),**
**thawed if frozen**
**4 to 6 fresh sage leaves (optional)**
**1 cup chicken broth**

1. Preheat oven to 325°F. Crumble sausage into large skillet. Add apple, shallot and celery; cook and stir over medium-high heat until sausage is cooked through and apple and vegetables are tender. Drain fat. Stir in hazelnuts, ¼ teaspoon each rubbed sage, salt and pepper. Spoon stuffing into shallow roasting pan.

2. Combine butter with remaining ¼ teaspoon each rubbed sage, salt and pepper. Spread over turkey breast skin. Arrange sage leaves under skin, if desired. Place rack on top of stuffing. Place turkey, skin side down, on rack. Pour broth into pan.

3. Roast turkey 45 minutes. Remove turkey from oven; turn skin side up. Baste with broth. Return to oven; roast 1 hour or until meat thermometer registers 165°F. Let turkey rest 10 minutes before carving. *Makes 6 servings*

# Rice Noodles with Broccoli & Tofu

**1 package (14 ounces) firm or extra-firm tofu**
**1 package (8 to 10 ounces) wide rice noodles**
**2 tablespoons peanut oil**
**3 medium shallots, sliced**
**6 cloves garlic, minced**
**1 jalapeño pepper,\* minced**
**2 teaspoons minced fresh ginger**
**3 cups broccoli florets**
**¼ cup gluten-free soy sauce**
**1 to 2 tablespoons fish sauce**
   **Fresh basil leaves (optional)**

*\*Jalapeño peppers can sting and irritate the skin, so wear rubber gloves when handling peppers and do not touch your eyes.*

1. Cut tofu crosswise into 2 pieces. Place tofu on cutting board between layers of paper towels; place weighted saucepan or baking dish on top of tofu. Let stand 30 minutes to drain. Place rice noodles in large bowl. Cover with boiling water; soak 30 minutes or until soft.

2. Cut tofu into bite-size squares and blot dry. Heat oil in large skillet or wok over medium-high heat. Add tofu to skillet; stir-fry about 5 minutes or until tofu is lightly browned on all sides. Remove from skillet.

3. Add shallots, jalapeño pepper, garlic and ginger to skillet. Stir-fry 2 to 3 minutes. Add broccoli; stir-fry 1 minute. Cover and cook 3 minutes or until broccoli is crisp-tender.

4. Drain noodles well; stir into skillet. Return tofu to skillet; add soy sauce and fish sauce. Stir-fry 8 minutes or until noodles are coated and flavors are blended. Adjust seasoning. Garnish with basil.

*Makes 4 to 6 servings*

# Cajun Chicken & Rice

**4 chicken drumsticks, skin removed**
**4 chicken thighs, skin removed**
**2 teaspoons Cajun seasoning**
**¾ teaspoon salt**
**2 tablespoons vegetable oil**
**1 can (about 14 ounces) chicken broth**
**1 cup uncooked rice**
**1 medium green bell pepper, coarsely chopped**
**1 medium red bell pepper, coarsely chopped**
**½ cup finely chopped green onions**
**2 cloves garlic, minced**
**½ teaspoon dried thyme**
**¼ teaspoon ground turmeric**

1. Preheat oven to 350°F. Lightly coat 13×9-inch baking dish with nonstick cooking spray; set aside.

2. Pat chicken dry. Sprinkle both sides with Cajun seasoning and salt. Heat oil in large skillet over medium-high heat. Add chicken; cook 8 to 10 minutes or until browned on all sides. Transfer to plate.

3. Add broth to skillet. Bring to a boil, scraping brown bits from bottom of skillet. Add rice, bell peppers, green onions, garlic, thyme and turmeric. Stir well. Pour into prepared baking dish. Place browned chicken on top. Cover tightly with foil. Bake 1 hour or until chicken is cooked through. *Makes 6 servings*

**Variation:** For a one-skillet meal, use an ovenproof skillet. Place browned chicken on mixture in skillet, cover and bake as directed.

# Two-Cheese Sausage Pizza

**1 pound sweet Italian turkey sausage**
**1 tablespoon olive oil**
**2 cups sliced mushrooms**
**1 small red onion, thinly sliced**
**1 small green bell pepper, cut into thin strips**
**¼ teaspoon salt**
**¼ teaspoon dried oregano**
**¼ teaspoon black pepper**
**½ cup pizza sauce**
**2 tablespoons tomato paste**
**½ cup shredded Parmesan cheese**
**1 cup (4 ounces) shredded mozzarella cheese**
**8 pitted ripe olives**

1. Preheat oven to 400°F. Remove sausage from casings. Pat into 9-inch glass pie plate. Bake 10 minutes or until sausage is firm. Carefully pour off fat. Set aside.

2. Heat oil in large skillet. Add mushrooms, onion, bell pepper, salt, oregano and black pepper. Cook and stir over medium-high heat 10 minutes or until vegetables are very tender.

3. Combine pizza sauce and tomato paste in small bowl; stir until well blended. Spread over sausage. Spoon half of vegetables over tomato sauce. Sprinkle with Parmesan and mozzarella cheeses. Top with remaining vegetables. Sprinkle with olives. Bake 8 to 10 minutes or until cheese melts. *Makes 4 servings*

# Southwest Spaghetti Squash

1 spaghetti squash (about 3 pounds)
1 can (about 14 ounces) Mexican-style diced tomatoes, undrained
1 can (about 14 ounces) black beans, rinsed and drained
¾ cup (3 ounces) shredded Monterey Jack cheese, divided
¼ cup finely chopped cilantro
1 teaspoon ground cumin
¼ teaspoon garlic salt
¼ teaspoon black pepper

1. Preheat oven to 350°F. Spray baking pan and 1½-quart baking dish with nonstick cooking spray. Cut squash in half lengthwise. Remove and discard seeds. Place squash, cut side down, in prepared baking pan. Bake 45 minutes to 1 hour or just until tender. Shred hot squash with fork; place in large bowl. (Use oven mitts to protect hands.)

2. Add tomatoes, beans, ½ cup cheese, cilantro, cumin, garlic salt and pepper; toss well. Spoon mixture into prepared dish. Sprinkle with remaining ¼ cup cheese.

3. Bake, uncovered, 30 to 35 minutes or until heated through. Serve immediately. *Makes 4 servings*

## *Tip

Spaghetti squash is a healthy gluten-free pasta substitute. If you don't have time to bake it, pierce the whole uncut squash with a knife and microwave it on HIGH 15 minutes or until tender. Let cool 10 minutes. Cut it in half, scoop out the seeds and shred squash with a fork.

# Better Birds

## Flourless Fried Chicken Tenders

**1½ cups chickpea flour***
**1½ teaspoons Italian seasoning**
  **1 teaspoon salt**
  **½ teaspoon black pepper**
  **⅛ teaspoon ground red pepper**
  **¾ cup plus 2 to 4 tablespoons water**
    **Oil for frying**
  **1 pound chicken tenders, cut in half if large**
    **Curry Mayo Dipping Sauce (recipe follows)**

*\*Chickpea flour is also called garbanzo flour. It is found in the specialty food section of most supermarkets.*

1. Sift chickpea flour into medium bowl. Stir in Italian seasoning, salt, black pepper and red pepper. Gradually whisk in ¾ cup water to make smooth batter. Whisk in additional water by tablespoons if needed until batter is consistency of heavy cream.

2. Meanwhile, add oil to large heavy skillet or Dutch oven to ¾-inch depth. Heat over medium-high heat until drop of batter placed in oil sizzles (350°F).

3. Pat chicken pieces dry. Dip pieces into batter with tongs; let excess fall back into bowl. Ease chicken gently into oil; fry 2 to 3 minutes per side until slightly browned and chicken is cooked through. Fry in batches; do not crowd pan.

4. Drain chicken on paper towels. Serve warm with Curry Mayo Dipping Sauce, if desired.               *Makes 4 servings*

**Curry Mayo Dipping Sauce:** Combine ½ cup mayonnaise, ¼ cup sour cream and ½ teaspoon curry powder in small bowl. Stir in 2 tablespoons minced fresh cilantro.

# Cornish Hens with Wild Rice & Pine Nut Pilaf

- **⅓ cup uncooked wild rice**
- **4 Cornish hens (about 1¼ pounds each)**
- **1 bunch green onions, cut into 2-inch pieces**
- **3 tablespoons olive oil, divided**
- **3 tablespoons gluten-free soy sauce**
- **⅓ cup pine nuts**
- **1 cup chopped onion**
- **1 teaspoon dried basil**
- **2 cloves garlic, minced**
- **2 jalapeño peppers,\* seeded and minced**
- **½ teaspoon salt**
- **Black pepper**

*\*Jalapeño peppers can sting and irritate the skin; wear rubber gloves when handling peppers and do not touch your eyes.*

1. Preheat oven to 425°F. Cook rice according to package directions.

2. Stuff hens equally with green onions; place hens on rack in roasting pan. Roast 15 minutes. Meanwhile, combine 1 tablespoon oil and soy sauce in small bowl. Baste hens with 1 tablespoon soy sauce mixture; roast 15 minutes or until cooked through (165°F). Baste with remaining soy sauce mixture. Let stand 15 minutes.

3. Heat large skillet over medium-high heat; add pine nuts. Cook 2 minutes or until golden, stirring constantly. Transfer to plate.

4. Add 1 tablespoon oil, onion and basil to same skillet. Cook 5 minutes or until browned, stirring frequently. Add garlic; cook 15 seconds, stirring constantly. Remove from heat. Add rice, pine nuts, jalapeño peppers, remaining 1 tablespoon oil and salt. Season with black pepper; toss gently to blend. Serve hens with rice mixture. *Makes 4 servings*

# Indian-Style Apricot Chicken

  6 chicken thighs
  ¼ teaspoon salt
  ¼ teaspoon black pepper
  1 tablespoon vegetable oil
  1 large onion, chopped
  2 tablespoons grated fresh ginger
  2 cloves garlic, minced
  ½ teaspoon ground cinnamon
  ⅛ teaspoon ground allspice
  1 can (14½ ounces) diced tomatoes, undrained
  1 cup chicken broth
  1 package (8 ounces) dried apricots
  1 pinch saffron threads (optional)
   Hot basmati rice
  2 tablespoons chopped fresh parsley (optional)

## Slow Cooker Directions

1. Coat slow cooker with nonstick cooking spray. Season chicken with salt and pepper. Heat oil in large skillet over medium-high heat; brown chicken on all sides. Transfer to slow cooker.

2. Add onion to skillet. Cook and stir 3 to 5 minutes or until translucent. Stir in ginger, garlic, cinnamon and allspice. Cook and stir 15 to 30 seconds or until mixture is fragrant. Add tomatoes with juice and broth. Cook 2 to 3 minutes or until heated through. Pour into slow cooker.

3. Add apricots and saffron, if desired. Cover; cook on LOW 5 to 6 hours or on HIGH 3 to 3½ hours or until chicken is tender. Serve with basmati rice and garnish with parsley.

*Makes 4 to 6 servings*

# Turkey with Pecan-Cherry Stuffing

**1 fresh or frozen boneless turkey breast (about 3 to 4 pounds)**
**2 cups cooked rice**
**⅓ cup chopped pecans**
**⅓ cup dried cherries or cranberries**
**1 teaspoon poultry seasoning**
**¼ cup peach, apricot or plum preserves**
**1 teaspoon Worcestershire sauce**

## Slow Cooker Directions

1. Thaw turkey breast, if frozen. Remove and discard skin. Cut slices three fourths of the way through turkey at 1-inch intervals.

2. Stir together rice, pecans, cherries and poultry seasoning in large bowl. Stuff rice mixture between slices. If needed, skewer turkey lengthwise to hold it together.

3. Place turkey in slow cooker. Cover; cook on LOW 5 to 6 hours or until turkey registers 165°F on meat thermometer inserted into thickest part of breast, not touching stuffing.

4. Stir together preserves and Worcestershire sauce. Spoon over turkey. Cover; let stand 5 minutes. *Makes 8 servings*

**Serving Suggestion:** Serve with asparagus spears and a spinach salad.

# Indian-Inspired Chicken with Raita

**1 cup plain yogurt**
**2 cloves garlic, minced**
**1 teaspoon salt**
**1 teaspoon ground coriander**
**1 teaspoon ground ginger**
**½ teaspoon ground turmeric**
**½ teaspoon ground cinnamon**
**½ teaspoon ground cumin**
**¼ teaspoon ground red pepper**
**1 (5- to 6-pound) chicken, cut into 8 pieces (about 4 pounds chicken parts)**

**Raita**

**2 medium cucumbers (about 1 pound), peeled, seeded and thinly sliced**
**⅓ cup plain yogurt**
**2 tablespoons chopped fresh cilantro**
**1 clove garlic, minced**
**¼ teaspoon salt**
**⅛ teaspoon black pepper**

1. Mix yogurt, garlic, salt, coriander, ginger, turmeric, cinnamon, cumin and red pepper in medium bowl. Place chicken in large resealable food storage bag. Add yogurt mixture; marinate in refrigerator 4 to 24 hours, turning occasionally.

2. Preheat broiler. Cover baking sheet with foil. Place chicken on prepared baking sheet. Broil 6 inches from heat about 30 minutes or until cooked through, turning once.

3. Meanwhile, prepare Raita. Mix cucumbers, yogurt, cilantro, garlic, salt and pepper in small bowl. Serve with chicken.

*Makes 6 to 8 servings*

# South American Chicken & Quinoa

**Tomato-Apricot Chutney (recipe follows)**
**1 teaspoon ground turmeric**
**1 teaspoon dried thyme**
**¾ teaspoon salt, divided**
**1 pound boneless skinless chicken breasts, cut into 1-inch pieces**
**2 tablespoons olive oil, divided**
**1 large green bell pepper, chopped**
**1 medium onion, chopped**
**1 cup uncooked quinoa**
**1 cup chicken broth**
**1 cup unsweetened coconut milk**
**1 teaspoon curry powder**
**¼ teaspoon ground ginger**

1. Prepare Tomato-Apricot Chutney; set aside.

2. Combine turmeric, thyme and ¼ teaspoon salt in shallow dish. Dip chicken pieces into spice mixture, coating all sides; set aside.

3. Heat 1 tablespoon oil in large skillet over medium-high heat. Add bell pepper and onion. Cook and stir 2 minutes or until vegetables are crisp-tender. Remove from skillet with slotted spoon; set aside.

4. Add remaining 1 tablespoon oil to skillet. Add chicken pieces. Cook and stir 5 minutes or until browned and chicken is cooked through.

5. Rinse quinoa in fine-mesh strainer under cold running water; drain well.

6. Combine quinoa, chicken broth, coconut milk, curry, remaining ½ teaspoon salt and ginger in large saucepan. Bring to a boil over high heat. Reduce heat to low; simmer, covered, 10 minutes.

7. Stir in chicken and pepper mixture; cook 5 minutes or until liquid is absorbed. Serve with Tomato-Apricot Chutney.

*Makes 4 servings*

# Tomato-Apricot Chutney

**¾ cup apple cider or apple juice**
**¾ cup finely diced dried apricots**
**½ cup currants or golden raisins**
**3 to 4 tablespoons cider vinegar**
**1 can (14½ ounces) diced tomatoes, drained**
**1 tablespoon dark brown sugar**
**1 teaspoon ground ginger**
**⅛ teaspoon ground cloves**

1. Combine apple cider, apricots, currants and vinegar in small saucepan. Bring to a boil over high heat. Reduce heat to low; simmer, covered, 10 minutes.

2. Stir in tomatoes, brown sugar, ginger and cloves; simmer, uncovered, 5 minutes or until liquid is absorbed.

*Makes about 3 cups*

# Pesto-Coated Baked Chicken

**1 pound boneless skinless chicken cutlets (½ inch thick)**
**¼ cup plus 1 tablespoon prepared pesto**
**1½ teaspoons sour cream**
**1½ teaspoons mayonnaise**
**1 tablespoon shredded Parmesan cheese**
**1 tablespoon pine nuts**

1. Preheat oven to 450°F. Arrange chicken in single layer in shallow baking pan. Combine pesto, sour cream and mayonnaise in small cup. Brush over chicken. Sprinkle with cheese and pine nuts.

2. Bake 8 to 10 minutes or until chicken is no longer pink in center.

*Makes 4 servings*

# Turkey
## Piccata

2½ **tablespoons rice flour**
¼ **teaspoon salt**
¼ **teaspoon black pepper**
1 **pound turkey breast, cut into short strips**
1 **tablespoon butter**
1 **tablespoon olive oil**
½ **cup chicken broth**
  **Grated peel of 1 lemon**
2 **teaspoons lemon juice**
2 **tablespoons finely chopped parsley**
2 **cups cooked rice**

### Slow Cooker Directions

1. Combine rice flour, salt and pepper in resealable food storage bag. Add turkey strips and shake well to coat. Heat butter and oil in large skillet over medium-high heat. Add turkey strips in single layer. Brown on all sides, about 2 minutes per side. Arrange in single layer in slow cooker.

2. Pour broth into skillet. Cook and stir to scrape up any browned bits. Pour into slow cooker. Add lemon peel and juice. Cover; cook on LOW 2 hours. Sprinkle with parsley before serving. Serve over rice. *Makes 4 servings*

### *Tip

It's a shame to limit turkey to Thanksgiving Day. Now that turkey breasts, turkey tenders and other fresh cuts are available all year long, try substituting turkey in your favorite chicken recipe. Turkey is lean, flavorful and an excellent source of protein.

# Orange-Almond Chicken

6 boneless skinless chicken breasts
Salt and black pepper
1½ cups sliced almonds
2 tablespoons rice flour
Grated peel of 1 medium orange (about 2 teaspoons)
1 egg
2 tablespoons water
2 to 4 tablespoons olive oil
Juice of 2 medium oranges (about ½ cup)
¾ cup chicken broth
1 tablespoon Dijon mustard
Additional grated orange peel and almonds (optional)

1. Cover chicken breasts with plastic wrap and pound to ¼-inch thickness; season with salt and pepper. Place almonds and rice flour in food processor; process using on/off pulsing action until coarse crumbs form. Add orange peel and pulse to combine.

2. Lightly beat egg and water in shallow bowl. Place almond mixture on plate. Coat chicken breasts in egg and then in almond mixture, pressing to make almond coating stick.

3. Heat 2 tablespoons oil in large skillet over medium-high heat. Cook chicken in batches without crowding skillet until lightly browned and no longer pink in center, about 5 minutes per side. Keep warm.

4. Add orange juice to same skillet; cook and stir until reduced by about half, scraping up brown bits on bottom of skillet. Add chicken broth and mustard; cook and stir 2 to 3 minutes. Pour over chicken. Garnish with additional orange peel and almonds, if desired. *Makes 6 servings*

**Serving Suggestion:** Serve with buttered French-cut green beans.

# Snacks & Treats

## Flourless Peanut Butter Cookies

**1 cup packed light brown sugar**
**1 cup smooth peanut butter**
**1 egg, lightly beaten**
**½ cup semisweet chocolate chips, melted**

**1.** Preheat oven to 350°F. Beat brown sugar, peanut butter and egg in medium bowl until blended and smooth.

**2.** Shape dough into 24 balls; place 2 inches apart on ungreased cookie sheets. Flatten slightly with fork. Bake 10 to 12 minutes or until set. Transfer to wire rack; cool completely. Drizzle with chocolate. *Makes 2 dozen cookies*

## Flourless Almond Cookies

**1 cup sugar**
**1 cup almond butter**
**1 egg, lightly beaten**

**1.** Preheat oven to 350°F. Beat sugar, almond butter and egg in large bowl with electric mixer until well combined.

**2.** Shape dough into 24 balls; place 2 inches apart on ungreased cookie sheets. Flatten slightly with fork.

**3.** Bake 10 minutes or until set. Transfer to wire rack; cool completely. *Makes 2 dozen cookies*

# Cranberry-Orange Rice Pudding

1 cup uncooked rice
1 tablespoon grated orange peel
1½ cups dried cranberries, coarsely chopped
½ cup orange juice
1 quart (4 cups) milk
1 can (12 ounces) evaporated milk
⅔ cup sugar
⅛ teaspoon salt

1. Cook rice according to package directions adding orange peel.

2. Meanwhile, combine cranberries and orange juice in medium saucepan; bring to a simmer over medium heat. Simmer 7 minutes or until juice is absorbed. Set aside.

3. Add milk, evaporated milk, sugar and salt to cooked rice. Cook and stir over medium-low heat about 40 minutes or until slightly thickened.

4. Stir cranberries into rice mixture. Cool to room temperature. Cover; refrigerate. Let stand at room temperature 10 minutes before serving.

*Makes 8 servings*

\*Tip

Chances are, if your diet is gluten-free you're eating more rice. It's a tasty carbohydrate that can fill in for flour-based pastas and starches. It's a great opportunity to enjoy some of the many different kinds of rice now readily available. Your supermarket probably stocks brown rice, basmati rice, long grain rice, jasmine rice and others.

# Almond Flour Pound Cake

½ **cup (1 stick) butter, softened**
½ **cup (4 ounces) cream cheese, softened**
¾ **cup sugar**
4 **eggs**
1 **teaspoon vanilla**
2 **cups almond flour***
1 **teaspoon baking powder**
½ **teaspoon salt**
¼ **teaspoon ground ginger**
¼ **teaspoon ground cardamom**
1 **tablespoon honey roasted sliced almonds**
**Berries and whipped cream (optional)**

*Almond flour, also called almond meal, is available at natural foods stores and in the specialty flour section at many supermarkets.*

1. Preheat oven to 350°F. Spray 9×5-inch loaf pan (or 2 mini loaf pans) with nonstick cooking spray.

2. Beat butter, cream cheese and sugar in large bowl with electric mixer until well blended.

3. Add eggs, one at a time, beating after each addition. Beat in vanilla.

4. Combine almond flour, baking powder, salt, ginger and cardamom in medium bowl. Gradually add to egg mixture while beating on medium speed.

5. Pour into prepared pan; sprinkle with honey-roasted almonds. Bake 45 to 55 minutes or until toothpick inserted into center comes out clean. Serve with berries and whipped cream, if desired.

*Makes 9 (1-inch) slices*

# Mixed Berry Crisp

**6 cups mixed berries, thawed if frozen**
**¾ cup packed brown sugar, divided**
**¼ cup minute tapioca**
   **Juice of ½ lemon**
**1 teaspoon ground cinnamon**
**6 tablespoons cold butter, cut into pieces**
**½ cup rice flour**
**½ cup sliced almonds**

1. Preheat oven to 375°F. Grease sides and bottom of 8- or 9-inch square baking pan.

2. Place berries in large bowl. Add ¼ cup sugar, tapioca, lemon juice and cinnamon; stir until well combined. Let stand while preparing topping.

3. Place butter, remaining ½ cup sugar and rice flour in food processor. Pulse until coarse crumbs form. Add almonds; pulse until combined. (Leave some large pieces of almonds.)

4. Transfer berry mixture to prepared pan. Sprinkle topping over berries. Bake 20 to 30 minutes or until topping is browned and filling is bubbly.                      *Makes about 9 servings*

**\*Tip**

For a gluten-free fruit dessert, a crisp is considerably easier than a pie since you don't need to bother with making a special crust. This recipe uses minute tapioca as a thickening agent, but you could also use cornstarch or arrowroot.

# Flourless Chocolate Cake

**1 cup whipping cream**
**1 cup plus 2 tablespoons sugar**
**12 squares (1 ounce each) unsweetened chocolate, coarsely chopped**
**4 squares (1 ounce each) semisweet chocolate, coarsely chopped**
**6 eggs, at room temperature**
**½ cup strong coffee**
**¼ teaspoon salt**
**½ cup chopped walnuts, divided**

1. Set oven rack to middle position. Preheat oven to 350°F. Spray 8-inch round cake pan with nonstick cooking spray.

2. Beat cream with 2 tablespoons sugar in large bowl with electric mixer at high speed until soft peaks form; set aside.

3. Place unsweetened and semisweet chocolate in large microwavable bowl; microwave on HIGH 2 to 3 minutes or until chocolate is melted, stirring after 1 minute and at 30-second intervals after the first minute.

4. Beat eggs and remaining 1 cup sugar in large bowl with electric mixer at high speed about 7 minutes or until pale and thick. Add melted chocolate, coffee and salt to egg mixture; beat until well blended.

5. Fold whipped cream and ¼ cup walnuts into egg mixture. Spread in prepared pan; sprinkle with remaining ¼ cup walnuts. Place pan in large roasting pan; add enough hot water to roasting pan to reach halfway up side of cake pan. Bake 30 to 35 minutes or until set but still soft in center.

6. To unmold, loosen edge of cake with knife; place serving plate upside down over pan and invert.                 *Makes 12 servings*

# Spicy Roasted Chickpeas

**1 can (about 20 ounces) chickpeas**
**3 tablespoons olive oil**
**½ teaspoon salt**
**½ teaspoon black pepper**
**¾ to 1 tablespoon chili powder**
**⅛ to ¼ teaspoon ground red pepper**
**1 lime, cut into wedges**

1. Preheat oven to 400°F. Rinse chickpeas in colander; drain well, shaking colander to remove as much water as possible.

2. Combine chickpeas, olive oil, salt and black pepper in large bowl. Spread in single layer in 15×10-inch baking pan. Bake 15 minutes or until chickpeas begin to brown, shaking pan twice.

3. Sprinkle with chili powder and red pepper to taste; bake 5 minutes or until dark golden-red. Serve with lime wedges.

*Makes 4 servings*

# Snack Mix

**3 cups gluten-free rice cereal squares**
**3 cups popped popcorn**
**½ cup mixed nuts or peanuts**
**3 tablespoons vegetable oil**
**⅓ cup grated Parmesan cheese**
**2 teaspoons garlic salt**
**2 teaspoons chili powder**

1. Preheat oven to 350°F. Combine cereal, popcorn and nuts in large bowl. Drizzle with oil and stir to coat. Sprinkle with cheese, garlic salt and chili powder, stirring to coat evenly.

2. Spread mixture on large ungreased baking sheet. Bake 15 minutes, turning pan once. Store in airtight container.

*Makes about 6 servings*

# Chocolate Coconut Almond Macaroons

**1⅓ cups flaked sweetened coconut (3½-ounce can)**
**⅔ cup sugar**
**2 egg whites**
**½ teaspoon vanilla**
**¼ teaspoon almond extract**
**Pinch salt**
**4 ounces sliced almonds, coarsely crushed**
**20 whole almonds**
**Chocolate Ganache (recipe follows)**

**1.** Combine coconut, sugar, egg whites, vanilla, almond extract and salt in medium bowl; mix well. Fold in sliced almonds. Cover and refrigerate at least 1 hour or overnight.

**2.** Preheat oven to 350°F. Line baking sheet with parchment paper. Roll dough by tablespoonfuls into balls. Place 1 inch apart on prepared sheet. Press almond on top of each cookie. Bake 15 minutes or until light brown. Cool cookies 5 minutes on baking sheets. Transfer to wire rack; cool completely.

**3.** Meanwhile, prepare Chocolate Ganache; let cool 10 to 15 minutes.

**4.** Dip bottom of each cookie into ganache. Place cookies on clean parchment or waxed paper-lined baking sheet. Refrigerate until ganache is firm. Store covered in refrigerator.

*Makes 1½ dozen cookies*

**Chocolate Ganache:** Place ½ cup semisweet chocolate chips in shallow bowl. Heat ¼ cup whipping cream in small saucepan until bubbles form around edges. Pour cream over chocolate; let stand 5 minutes. Stir until smooth.

# Index